WORDS FROM YOUR SISTER

A SCRIPTURAL DEVOTIONAL

ANGELIA VERNON MENCHAN

October 2014©

HONORABLE MENCHAN MEDIA

This book is dedicated to all my sisters, by blood, design and heart. We are on this spiritual walk designed by God together.

All scriptures herein are from the English Standard Version Bible.

WORDS FROM YOUR SISTER   Angelia Vernon Menchan

Table of Contents

LOVE

    Page 5

FORGIVENESS

    Page 12

FAITH

    Page 19

MARRIAGE

    Page 23

FRIENDSHIP

    Page 29

FAMILY

    Page 32

ENDURANCE

    Page 35

HOPE

    Page 41

WORDS FROM YOUR SISTER   Angelia Vernon Menchan

HONESTY

> Page 45

CHURCH ATTENDANCE AND STUDY

> Page 50

WORDS FROM YOUR SISTER　　　Angelia Vernon Menchan

LOVE

1 John 4:7-8

Beloved, let us love one another, for love is from God, and whoever loves has been born of God and knows God. Anyone who does not love does not know God, because God is love

Why is it so difficult to show love to others?

We have all asked ourselves that question, surely. The answer is not simple and it can be complex but at the root of it, is our own flesh. We find it difficult to love others because we do not feel we are getting anything back.

The flesh will have us believe that we cannot love until we are loved. But the bible tells us clearly in many passages that is not true. God loves us even when we are unlovable and true Christian love, loves past our flesh.

We also have to realize that love is not just feelings and emotions. True love transcends that and is something we offer even in our struggles.

As a young girl, I hated my stepfather. He was mean to my mom and he did not care for me. At least I thought I hated him but as years rolled past and things changed I learned that I did not hate him and meant no ill will towards him, I just did not like how he was as a person and his values and how he dealt with his own inner issues.

I had to literally try to understand that this uneducated man who was raised to fight against skin color, a lack of education and racism was dealing with life with his fists because that was what he understood and more than hate, he needed love and compassion from others. From me! I am telling you that was more than a notion.

Many thought me crazy that I didn't bear grudges against him and allowed my children to have close relationships with him but to me that was freedom. We had moved past those things and through God loving me and forgiving me and my mess, I was able to forgive him and be at peace about what had transpired.

LUKE 6: 27-36

But I say to you who hear, Love your enemies, do good to those who hate you, bless those who curse you, pray for

WORDS FROM YOUR SISTER Angelia Vernon Menchan

those who abuse you. To one who strikes you on the cheek, offer the other also, and from one who takes away your cloak do not withhold your tunic either. Give to everyone who begs from you, and from one who takes away your goods do not demand them back. And as you wish that others would do to you, do so to them.

I know you are all saying, "Love my enemies and do good to them who hate you?" our sister, Angelia has fallen and bumped her head. She might be able to do that but I am not trying to love nobody who hated and cursed me and if she thinks for one minute, someone can strike my cheek and I not knock them out cold, she has another thought coming!

I know, I know, believe me I know.

I think sometimes we are too literal to be blessed. What God is commanding is that we not hold malice in our hearts and do not try to do wrong for wrong. We cannot and will not be blessed by God if we discover someone has slandered us and the first thing we do is go forth and slander them. Two wrongs still does not make things right and as children of the Most High, we must rise above commonality.

Is it easy?

No, my sisters it is not. It is something I learned as I lived. There was a time in my late teens and twenties when someone could say or do something to me and the looks I gave them and the sharp retorts left them quaking in my wake.

But, you know what? Ultimately, I did not feel any better. I struggled internally with the fact that I always had to exact my revenge through my words. Not only that, I developed something of a reputation and it took years to overcome. In fact to this day, people who have not seen me in decades still judge me based on those looks and retorts.

What I had to learn is that everything did not deserve a response and often a win for me was to say nothing. When I learned the power of silence and figuratively turning the other cheek, my life became more blessed and peaceful. I learned that it was more spiritually powerful to allow the devil to have his say without response. In many ways, I became a devil slayer by loving my enemies with silence and prayer. Because pray I did, to stop my tongue from taking control. Do I hit my marks every time? I am afraid not but more often than not; I can be blessed by being quiet, prayerful and loving.

1 CORINTHIANS 13-4-7

Love is patient and kind; love does not envy or boast; it is not arrogant or rude. It does not insist on its own way; it is not irritable or resentful; it does not rejoice at wrongdoing, but rejoices with the truth. Love bears all things, believes all, things, hopes all things, and endures all things.

Is your love patient and kind or does it demand things? Does it force you to say, 'If you really loved me, you would do such and such?"

Come on, be honest. We have all been there. We want those who profess to love us to show us and if it is not as we want it, we are neither patient nor kind. In fact, we can become surly and impatient, demanding to have love proven. That my sisters is not love, it is more commonly known as manipulation and can be a love deal breaker if we are not careful.

True love also does not boast or brag, show off or demean. We can often confuse honesty with being boastful or even rude. We have all encountered and at times been the sister who says, "I am doing this because I love you and I am just keeping it real with love."

Sure! What we are in fact doing in many cases is telling others how wonderful we are for loving them and telling them off and trying to dress it up, calling it love. I have been there and done that and received it as well.

No one wishes to be love manipulated and made to feel if they do not bend to our will they are not loving and they certainly have no desire to be crushed by that in your face 'love' that feels like a roller coaster.

We have to pray before speaking and professing love and in some cases, leave things unsaid until God has given us the right message and he always does. Something that helps me tremendously is remembering how I want to be loved and asking God to allow me to love others in the same way.

FORGIVENESS

EPHESIANS 4:32 ESV

Be kind to one another, tenderhearted, forgiving one another, as God in Christ forgave you.

Oh my Forgiveness…

That my sisters is one of the hardest things under the sun to do. But, is the most blessed when one is able to do it.

I have had so many conversations with people about this one and they will stare straight in my face and ask, 'How do you expect me to forgive a man who beat me, a mom who left me, a boss who mistreated me?'

I quickly tell them, I do not expect them to do anything but God expects it. Forgiving is mentioned throughout the bible and I am a living witness that forgiving is not just about the forgiven but about the forgiver.

For whatever reason, I am unable to bear a grudge. I have always said it is a flaw in me that I have learned to

WORDS FROM YOUR SISTER Angelia Vernon Menchan

embrace. For years, I truly wanted to. However, being an outspoken person who will tell a person they have hurt me, freed me from that in many ways.

On the flip side, I have had to forgive many for wrongs done to me and in some cases egregious wrongs, my mom for living with a man who was brutal to me, same man for his brutality and on…I have also had to be forgiven by those who are close to me, my husband and children for my sometimes laser sharp tongue and others who have felt my wrath.

Every morning, I thank God for allowing me to forgive people and move on with my life because the inability to forgive is much the same as filling one's body with bitter poison and walking through life each day, tasting and feeling the poison filtrate through your spirit and soul. More importantly, those we are unable to forgive have often gone on with their lives, living fully while we are barely able to move, consumed with our feelings.

Forgiveness frees the forgiver, I liken it to being released from prison and exonerated by God to live fully without bitterness, anger and malice.

Many ask does forgiving a person mean I have to allow them to continue to treat me badly, beat me up, and harm my spirit.

No, indeed it does not. We can love and forgive hurtful people from afar and often we must in order to live full lives.

Forgiveness has to start with a desire to let things go and to do so we must pray and immerse ourselves in the word daily. There are many times when I am sure people are concerned about the tall lady walking and talking to herself.

Let them think what they want. What I am doing is walking and talking to God, asking him to free me from my feelings so I can forgive those who have wronged and ask for forgiveness from those I have wronged and from God. I assure you He will do it.

2 TIMOTHY 3:16 ESV

All Scripture is breathed out by God and profitable for teaching, for reproof, for correction, and for training in righteousness

Matthew 6:9-13 ESV

Pray then like this: "Our Father in heaven, hallowed be your name. Your kingdom come, your will be done, on earth as it is in heaven. Give us this day our daily bread, and forgive us our debts, as we also have forgiven our debtors. And lead us not into temptation, but deliver us from evil.

HEBREWS 10:17 ESV

Then he adds, "I will remember their sins and their lawless deeds no more."

Stop looking at me like that, sisters!

I know you are saying it is one thing to forgive, but I am not Jesus and I cannot forget, I just can't."

I hear you!

That was one of my hardest lessons ever! If you don't believe me ask my husband. I would forgive but I never forgot and in the heat of the next 'discussion' my very clear memory would present itself, with dates times and what we were wearing.

When my husband would say, "You are always bringing up old stuff." I would roll my eyes and say, "I sure am and you don't want to hear the truth, shame on you!"

Sisters! I know you are feeling me there. It took me years to stop doing that with him and my sons. I was good at not doing it with others but the three of them, they heard it, sho did.

WORDS FROM YOUR SISTER   Angelia Vernon Menchan

Do you know what that meant?

It meant I had not truly forgiven but had banked it until they made me mad again, so I could tell them in full detail how wrong they were! Until, I learned to literally pray and ask God to remove that from my tongue and heart it continued. To this day when something occurs that is tied to some old mess, I have to stop in mid-sentence and ask God for strength not to go back there and drag up old mess.

Memories are rarely washed away but how we deal with them speaks to our walk with God and the closer and stronger our walk, the easier it becomes to leave those forgiven transgressions against us where they are buried. Sometimes, it is as simple as remembering we do not want to constantly hear about our sins against others, so why do we think they want to hear that from us. Amen and thank you Jesus!

PROVERBS 19:11 ESV

Good sense makes one slow to anger, and it is his glory to overlook an offense.

WORDS FROM YOUR SISTER   Angelia Vernon Menchan

FAITH

ROMANS 10:17 ESV

So faith comes from hearing, and hearing through the word of Christ

How does Faith come by hearing, one might ask?

Hearing the word of God from those ordained by him to preach it in an expository manner. It is easy to get the good word these days. Many preachers, prophets, bishops et al. are willing to give us a word. A word where they take a bit of scripture and add their own twists to it to make it palatable so we will feel good about ourselves and buy in.

Because surely we all want to hear that if we love God and have faith we can all have money, live in mansions, and drive Rolls Royce. But that is not what the word of God says. The bible tells is there will times of trials and tribulations and that believers will come under persecution. Every day will not be one filled with good times and happiness. We are being deceived by those who tell us we can name it and claim it or even speak it into existence. If you are praying for something that God does not think you need, you will not get that blessing from him. We have to remember to pray that His will is done in our lives. We may get those things but everything we receive is not from God and we must be mindful of who we are receiving from. Satan also gives rewards!

1 Peter 5:10 ESV

I have said these things to you, that in me you may have peace. In the world you will have tribulation. But take heart; I have overcome the world."

John 16:33 ESV

And after you have suffered a little while, the God of all grace, who has called you to his eternal glory in Christ, will himself restore, confirm, strengthen, and establish you

Romans 5:3 ESV

More than that, we rejoice in our sufferings, knowing that suffering produces endurance.

WORDS FROM YOUR SISTER   Angelia Vernon Menchan

True faith allows us to endure the trials and tribulations without losing our minds. We stay focused on the word of God and off what is going on in the world.

I can assure you there have been times of late when I have read the newspaper, or watched the news and if my faith in God were not real, I would lose my mind. Without faith it would be nearly impossible to understand and live through murder, mayhem and filth that is so currently pervasive. Faith and reliance on God and the Word keeps me steadfast.

Is every day filled with happiness?

Of course not, but if he brings me to it, he will bring me through it and I know and can testify to the times when I have been as low as it is possible to feel but through the cracks, I could see the sun shining and I kept my knees bent and my heart and soul lifted by being immersed in the Word and I was here to see another day.

Faith to me is the knowledge that as my elders used to say, God has his hands on you at all times and will give you no more than you can bear. That no matter how dark it is in the world, the light of God will make my personal path clear.

WORDS FROM YOUR SISTER Angelia Vernon Menchan

MARRIAGE

Matthew 19:6

So they are no longer two but one flesh. What therefore God has joined together; let not man separate.

At the writing of these words, I have been married thirty-six years and twenty five days but who is counting?

The verse above from Matthew has been my mainstay.

When my husband and I became engaged our marriage was not encouraged. For whatever reasons his family did not see me as wife material for him and made no bones about making sure I knew.

My mom didn't say much about it one way or the other but I know she felt I was trying to be as far away from her as possible and many of my friends felt that in my quiet studiousness and my fiancé in his less studious exuberance was not the perfect match but here we are.

What we had more than anything was love and devotion to the other and we both wanted something together we had never seen manifested. Also, God worked in our lives in a beautiful way that saved us and our marriage, for twenty two years we traveled the world in the military and was away from the potential line of fire from family and friends and their opinions and meddling. We were able to establish our marriage thousands of miles away.

We were married and raising our kids without input from anyone. When we struggled we struggled and left others out of our business. When we did not have money, we did not borrow we did without because you all know that people will try to own you with their money. At times we were not even attributing what we were doing to God because we did not have enough sense to do that but now we KNOW it was all God.

By the time we returned close to family we were as entrenched in our love and marriage as it was possible to be and no one was putting nothing asunder, thank you and hallelujah.

There are times when we can all use a little friendly advice but we have to be discerning about who we share our lives and marriage woes with. Everyone is not a blessing to your marital accord. Until we figured that out, we learned to keep our business to ourselves and at first muddle and love ourselves through and once we knew better we added God to our relationship and the twists became a tight braid and we were and are stronger for it.

There were times when we prayed separately, yes! But God showed us that praying together and vocally was more blessed. Marriage is no place to be too proud to pray together. It is a sad commentary on marriage, if a couple cannot share their prayer life. We all need private time with God but at the risk of being cliché, a family who prays together, often stays together. Amen!

Genesis 2:24 ESV

Therefore a man shall leave his father and his mother and hold fast to his wife, and they shall become one flesh

Ephesians 5:20-29 ESV

Giving thanks always and for everything to God the Father in the name of our Lord Jesus Christ, submitting to one another out of reverence for Christ. Wives, submit to your own husbands, as to the Lord. For the husband is the head of the wife even as Christ is the head of the church, his body, and is himself its Savior. Now as the church submits to Christ, so also wives should submit in everything to their husbands

Folks don't like that submit part. Women get up in arms when they hear it and necks swirl.

"I ain't submitting to no man!" Umm hmm.

I hear you but the word say to submit to our husbands as he submits to God. I promise you if your man is submissive to God, submitting to him is a blessed thing indeed. Submission does not mean being trampled upon or treated badly, some wives and husbands are using submission out of biblical context. We submit through loving him, respecting him, recognizing that God has placed him as head of your household. As an aside, I once heard a pastor say, "Women submit to worthy men."

So… when choosing a man, we might want to make sure he is worthy of our love, respect and submission.

Ephesians 5:33 ESV

However, let each one of you love his wife as himself, and let the wife see that she respects her husband.

Marriage is work. There are no days off from marital work. Each morning before my feet hit the floor after thanking God for loving and keeping me and all the many blessings, he continually bestow upon me, I ask him to keep my marriage strong and do whatever it takes to do that.

Lord,

Please still my tongue and open my ears so I can hear you and what my husband has to say before I respond. If I am in disagreement about something allow me to meditate on it before saying anything. During my day, keep my heart, mind and eyes focused on you and my marriage so my frail mind won't wander where it should not and keep all negative words against my husband and marriage out of my mouth when speaking to others because what I say is as much a reflection of me as it is of him.

Amen

FRIENDSHIP

PROVERBS 17-17 ESV

Friends love through all kinds of weather, and families stick together in all kinds of trouble

PROVERBS 27-17

You use steel to sharpen steel, and one friend sharpens another.

I love my friends and I never use the word friend lightly. There are women in my life who are spiritual and honest and they trust me to pray for them and likewise. And a praying friend is a friend indeed.

These are women who know my heart and still love me! I can be myself with them at all times and I know that while they applaud my successes, they will call me on my messes. More than anything, they correct me with loving, strong words directly from the word of God.

WORDS FROM YOUR SISTER   Angelia Vernon Menchan

Anyone can say something pretty and make us feel better. Or something not so pretty in trying to 'empower' us.

One on the phrases, I just do not care for is a sister-girl mantra in some places:

"I can do bad all by myself!"

Ugh! Whenever I hear that mess I cringe. I totally understand what they are saying, "If I am going to have a man he needs to do something for me, otherwise I can do bad all by myself." Did, I say ugh!

That is such a bitter and negative statement and whenever I hear my friends making statements like that, we talk, yes we do.

What we as women of faith should be saying is, "With Christ, I can do well because I know he covers and cares for me even I when I am lonely, broken and do not have a husband."

Words are mighty powerful and I kid you not, if enough men hear those words from your mouth, especially if your mouth is twisted and neck swirling, they will leave you to do just that, bad all by yourself.

True friends love and support each other; we are also lovingly honest and keep each other on spiritual and godly paths. We do not condone our friends' foolishness. A friend know she cannot come to me and say she is cheating on her husband and have me say, "Girl, I understand. Things happen." She will be lovingly reminded that God does not bless that mess. I expect the same from my friends. I implore them to not let me go astray with foolishness. If you are my friend, you will sit me down and straighten me out.

- ***Proverbs 13:20 ESV***

   Become wise by walking with the wise; hang out with fools and watch your life fall to pieces.

FAMILY

COLLOSIANS 3:13 ESV

Bearing with one another and, if one has a complaint against another, forgiving each other; as the Lord has forgiven you, so you also must forgive.

Bearing with one another is right. Whew. Family is that group of people we love most and with that love comes a multitude of sins. Honey, we know our people and they know us and often we do not let them forget we know them and they know us. We take every chance we get when they come up against us to remind them.

There was a time in my life when my sister, my only sister and I were struggling and the first words from her mouth were, "They don't know you like I know you!" and she was not complimenting me.

WORDS FROM YOUR SISTER   Angelia Vernon Menchan

She was absolutely right. They don't know me as she knew me. But, I am no longer that woman who would lash out and cuss you out, cutting you cold with a look. We had not lived in the same hometown in decades when she made that statement and the truth as I told her was neither of us knew each other as women. Our lives had been changed and transformed by our experiences, travels, troubles and relationships and mostly we were like ships passing.in the night.

I told her, "You don't know me, you knew me and I don't know you."

That Labor Day conversation changed the course of our relationship because as hard as the words were we knew we had to start from where we were as women and not destroys each other with words from the past.

To this day, I have family members, friends and elders who discuss old hurts from over fifty years ago as if they just occurred. They are mired down in it and are not trying to bear anything or forgive anyone. Bless their hearts.

Family is the one place that many of us can never leave and we never want to but we have to learn how to be honest with compassion and remember God is our family first and foremost and if he can put up with our wretched mess, then surely we can learn to coexist with some peace and compassion with our earthly families. Surely?

<u>2 Corinthians 6:18</u> ESV

And I will be a father to you, and you shall be sons and daughters to me, says the Lord Almighty."

<u>Deuteronomy 26:11</u> ESV

And you shall rejoice in all the good that the Lord your God has given to you and to your house, you, and the Levite, and the sojourner who is among us.

ENDURANCE

ROMANS 5:3-5 ESV

More than that, we rejoice in our sufferings, knowing that suffering produces endurance, and endurance produces character, and character produces hope, and hope does not put us to shame, because God's love has been poured into our hearts through the Holy Spirit who has been given to us.

Recently my youngest son was going through on his job. He came home and told me, they were testing him and out to get him. I stopped chopping vegetables and looked him square in the face.

"Perhaps they are. We are all tested and since your dad is the director, maybe they are trying to see if you are made of the same stuff."

I saw a bit of a light come on in his eyes. I said to him, "Endurance gives you strength."

Winking at me as he walked from the kitchen, he said, "In that case, I should be able to bench press a Buick."

I howled with laughter at that and felt his pain. I have endured some things in my life that should have taken me right out of the game of life. There have been days when it took all I could to get out of bed because it seemed like it was one thing after the other.

January, 2003, I lost my mother after a courageous battle with breast cancer. When she was diagnosed in 1998, they had not expected her to live but a few months but she lived almost five years.

I moved back to Florida in 1999 and for four years we watched the literal life seep out of her. It was hard to watch and it was hard on my relationships. My sister and I were at odds and I am sure there were times my husband was not thrilled with the time I had to go back and forth to Ocala to care for her, to top it off my youngest was fourteen to seventeen and crazy as a teenager.

WORDS FROM YOUR SISTER Angelia Vernon Menchan

By the time mama died, I was numb and filled with guilt about what I had not done and if what I had done was enough. For months, I moved through life as if an automaton. What I really wanted to do was get in my Camry and go to Maine, leaving home, hearth, husband and children in my wake. I prayed much.

Before I could start to feel like me again, my godmother who was over one hundred years old died, exactly a year later. This was a woman who was in the room with mama, me and the midwife when I was delivered and who had loved me completely. She taught me so many practical things. I was sure I was going to become a bottle of delicious wine because I felt crushed by life and all things.

I was also in a job with increased pressure and turmoil was my friend.

One day in late 2004 I sat in my doctor's office and tears poured. She asked if I were okay and I unloaded. Touching my shoulder, she listened with compassion and actually prayed for me.

WORDS FROM YOUR SISTER　　　Angelia Vernon Menchan

"My dear, you are grieving. You have suffered so much loss and you carry yourself with such dignity." She said.

I looked at her because I felt anything but dignified but I had been raised to never let them see me sweat. She told me I needed to allow myself to feel and get past things and she prescribed me a mild anti-depressant for thirty days.

I went home and spoke to my husband and was further surprised by his words.

"Baby, you take all this on yourself. You do everything for everyone and you really don't have to. That is you. You also allow us to make you feel guilty when you don't do things and you need to stop that.'"

I looked at him as if he had three heads. Who was this guy?

But I knew he was right. Since I was a young girl, I had taken on the role of enduring martyr. When my stepfather hit my mom, I was her protector, when someone messed with my sister and later my sons, I fought their battles. My husband was a professional soldier and was often gone and

WORDS FROM YOUR SISTER Angelia Vernon Menchan

in his absence and sometimes his presence I took on all things.

"Baby, you are going to have to let some things go."

He pulled me in his arms and held me until I cried out and fell asleep. I took several days off and got into the word of God and allowed myself to slowly heal. I say slowly because there are some days, I still want to strap an S to my chest and solve the worlds issues but I know I cannot. I know that is why I have God and the man he gave me and those wonderful friends to lean and rely on. I am an endurer to be sure but I don't have to endure alone. Thank God for that!

Romans 5:1-21 ESV /

Therefore, since we have been justified by faith, we have peace with God through our Lord Jesus Christ. Through him we have also obtained access by faith into this grace in which we stand, and we rejoice in hope of the glory of God. More than that, we rejoice in our sufferings, knowing that suffering produces endurance, and endurance produces character, and character produces

hope, and hope does not put us to shame, because God's love has been poured into our hearts through the Holy Spirit who has been given to us.

James 1:2-4 ESV

Count it all joy, my brothers, when you meet trials of various kinds, for you know that the testing of your faith produces steadfastness. And let steadfastness have its full effect, that you may be perfect and complete, lacking in nothing.

HOPE

PSALMS 39-7

"And now, O Lord, for what do I wait? My hope is in you.

There is nothing sadder to me than to encounter someone without hope. Hope is what keeps us strong and looking forward after love and faith. There are times when I am driving along Main Street and I see the drunks, drug addicts, prostitutes and others who seem so lost and hopeless and I wonder what transpired to get them to that darkest place.

I remember living on 20th Avenue in Ocala, Florida from age nine to twelve and those were rough years. It was what would come to be known as 'the hood' and it was filled with all kinds of people. There were a great many that had come to that place where they lived as if all hope were gone. Most of their days were filled with alcohol, promiscuous sex and violence. Every single day I rubbed up against it. There are times when I return to my hometown and I drive past that green stone house that still sits on the corner. When you walked in there was a living room and kitchen that led to a screened in back porch. There were also two bedrooms separated by a bathroom. That was the house where my mom and stepfather started living together and inside those walls I saw violence and was often afraid but for some reason I never felt hopeless.

There were days when I walked to school laughing with my friends and the next day those same friends would gang up and fight me for varied reasons. I also saw many of my young friends succumb to young sexual experience and motherhood in their teens, I saw others go to and fro to jail for myriad reasons and I saw people literally stand in the street and cuss God. But I never felt hopeless.

I now know that is because God always kept his hands on me. He gifted me to be a good student and also gave me a mom that no matter what she went through she also kept her hands on me and kept me on a straight path. I knew doing poorly in school, having sex as a child or going out

WORDS FROM YOUR SISTER Angelia Vernon Menchan

in the streets was not an option for me. In addition to my mom, there were my godmother, aunts, teachers and others who looked out for my best interests. And that gave me hope in really dark places.

When I was twelve and starting seventh grade we moved away from that area and in essence I never looked back. Whenever I encountered people from that time in my life, I acknowledged them, spoke and talked but kept moving and doing what I was here to do.

There are times to this day when I encounter them and they tell me they are proud of me for getting out and staying out. They attribute it to my being smart but it was way more than a twelve year old brain. God removed his child from that situation because he had work for me to do. He was working on and in me when I did not have a clue.

During that time I was largely unchurched but I read the bible every day. I Corinthians, Psalms and Proverbs were my biblical reading material and they provided me calm in many a storm. There were times when I would crawl into my twin bed in that dark room and read those scriptures over and over until I feel asleep, sirens and harsh words twirling around me. The Word was truly my refuge and allowed me to always stay hopeful and hope filled.

Romans 8:24 ESV /

For in this hope we were saved. Now hope that is seen is not hope. For who hopes for what he sees?

Jeremiah 17:7 ESV

"Blessed is the man who trusts in the Lord, whose trust is the Lord.

Psalm 71:14 ESV

But I will hope continually and will praise you yet more and more

HONESTY

PROVERBS 12:22

Lying lips are an abomination to the Lord, but those who act faithfully are his delight.

Growing up my mama used to say, "She who lies will also, steal and cheat." I thought at that time mama was saying too much."

Just because I told a story (we weren't allowed to say lying when I was growing up, that was considered cussing) about not eating the jellyroll, didn't mean I was going to steal and cheat.

I was given a jellyroll by my godmother and told I could not eat it until after supper. Now, you have to understand how much I loved a jellyroll. That soft cake, filled with strawberry jelly all rolled up and covered with coconut. Yes!

Anyway, at age four or five, she gave me the jellyroll and they went on to discuss grow folks business. After staring at it for a long time, I carefully un-wrapped it, bit a nice chunk and folded it up. At the end of the evening when my godmother was leaving, she asked, "Baby, did you bite that jellyroll or did a mice get in and bite it?"

Immediately, I saw my out and said, "A mice did."

She stared at me for several minutes and took the package from me. It was as if she was giving me time to confess my lie. Of course I didn't and she took the treat and placed in in the garbage can with fish scales and other stuff, pushing it down. I stared at her in horror; sure she was losing her very mind. Who does that to a perfect jellyroll? She then threw ashes from the ashtray on top. Tears filled my eyes. Looking at me again, she said, "I would never want you to eat behind a dirty mouse."

I was bereft and convinced she had lost her mind and my jellyroll at the same time. Later my mom told me if I had told the truth, I would have gotten in a bit of trouble for not doing what I was told but because I lied I lost my favorite dessert. It was a long time before I ever ate

WORDS FROM YOUR SISTER   Angelia Vernon Menchan

another jellyroll but it was a lesson I never forgot and still resonates five decades later.

There have been many times in my life when I was told I was too honest. There really is no such thing as too honest but what I learned was I was too harsh with my truth.

I had to learn to temper what I say without destroying a person with my words but to maintain integrity at the same time. I also learned that honesty can also involve keeping one's mouth closed. Also as adults we must be careful how we model honesty to children.

When I was six I was living in New Jersey with my mom and aunt and one Sunday we were standing outside before church. Their friend strolled towards them and she was wearing a loud colored dress full of flowers and had a hat on her head that was a literal bowl of fruit. My mom and aunt exchanged looks.

"Girl, she looks like a fool with all that on her head and it don't even go with that loud suit." Auntie whispered. Mama shook her head in agreement.

"I know that's right, I know Carmen Miranda is turning over in her grave. She looks a sight."

When the friend got close, of course she pranced around asking how she looked. Immediately they both said, "Oh child, you know you looking good today. Go on now." I looked at them both in shock.

"But mama, y'all said…" before the other words could leave my mouth, mama yanked my skin in a hard pinch, bringing tears to my eyes. I was so confused. I had been told not to lie but they had just stood in that lady's face and did just that. That was my introduction to, "Do as I say, not as I do, "from grown folks. Umph, Umph, Umph.

The bottom line truth is people, especially children learn from what we do and not what we say. Amen!

Proverbs 6:16-20 ESV

There are six things that the Lord hates, seven that are an abomination to him: haughty eyes, a lying tongue, and hands that shed innocent blood, a heart that devises wicked plans, feet that make haste to run to evil, a false witness who breathes out lies, and one who sows discord among brothers. My sons, keep your father's commandment, and forsake not your mother's teaching

John 8:32 ESV

And you will know the truth, and the truth will set you free."

Philippians 4:8-9 ESV

Finally, brothers, whatever is true, whatever is honorable, whatever is just, whatever is pure, whatever is lovely, whatever is commendable, if there is any excellence, if there is anything worthy of praise, think about these things. What you have learned and received and heard and seen in me—practice these things, and the God of peace will be with you.

Church Attendance and Studying the Bible

Hebrews 10:24-25

And let us consider how to stir up one another to love and good works, not neglecting to meet together, as is the habit of some, but encouraging one another, and all the more as you see the Day drawing near.

If I had a nickel for every time I heard some say I don't need to attend church to praise the Lord. I would be nickel rich. I have said it at times in my life. But I am here to tell you and I can only speak for me, when I was left to my own devices I didn't always praise The Lord. I need church and fellowship to keep me grounded. I also need an expository preacher to explain and expound upon the scriptures so I can better understand it. I can read the bible but I never learned the word until I joined the church and sat under bible believing preachers and studied the word with understanding. Reading is one things and understanding another.

ROMANS 10:17 ESV

So faith comes from hearing, and hearing through the word of Christ

I can read for hours on end and glean some things but there is nothing like sitting under the word of God with likeminded individuals who yearn for truth and understanding. The more the word is spoken, the more I understand and I am not ashamed to admit I am not able to do it or understand it under my own power. I also need those I can call on for guidance who have also been taught. I need church and fellowship to keep me and my house in order.

I also need personal study time. After the word has been preached and taught, I need to read the scriptures for myself, asking God for understanding so I can make his words applicable to my life.

There are times when I must go to a quiet place and allow the words of God to flow down upon me to give me peace. The world is full of trials and at the end of the day of navigating my way through corporate and governmental angst, not to mention humans and traffic, there is nothing like the word of Jesus to quench my thirsty soul.

God and his words deliver and being in corporate worship with other believers is food for my weary and word starved soul. I am unable to do any of this with guidance, teaching and the unfiltered, unaltered word of God.

1 John 1:7 ESV

But if we walk in the light, as he is in the light, we have fellowship with one another, and the blood of Jesus his Son cleanses us from all sin.

Psalm 150:1-6 ESV

Praise the Lord! Praise God in his sanctuary; praise him in his mighty heavens! Praise him for his mighty deeds; praise him according to his excellent greatness! Praise him with trumpet sound; praise him with lute and harp! Praise him with tambourine and dance; praise him with strings and pipe! Praise him with sounding cymbals; praise him with loud clashing cymbals!

1 John 1:7 ESV

But if we walk in the light, as he is in the light, we have fellowship with one another, and the blood of Jesus his Son cleanses us from all sin.

Psalm 150:1-6 ESV

Praise the Lord! Praise God in his sanctuary; praise him in his mighty heavens! Praise him for his mighty deeds; praise him according to his excellent greatness! Praise him with trumpet sound; praise him with lute and harp! Praise him with tambourine and dance; praise him with strings and pipe! Praise him with sounding cymbals; praise him with loud clashing cymbals!

I love the word of God and I love attending church with those who do likewise. I know folks say the church is full of hypocrites. Of course it is, we come to church from the world. Church is not a showplace for saints but a hospital for the lost so we can all learn and be washed clean by the blood.

I have been churched and unchurched and I assure you churched has been better for me, mind, body and soul and better for my marriage and my interactions with other humans.

That's not to say that going to church guarantees you will get to heaven; that is based upon your acceptance of Jesus Christ as your savior.

If you are struggling; feeling lost and all alone, try church and start to immerse yourself in the truth, the holy word of God and I tell you, if you give yourself fully to being saved, you and your life will be changed. I know for a fact if Jesus saved me, there is hope for all of us. There will be times of trials but during the worst of them, you might not be happy but you can find JOY! Happiness is that thing that depends on people and things and when they aren't there we suffer, but JOY is what sustains us even in the midst of our going through. We learn to smile through our tears because we know God promised us another day.

JUST LOVE and BLESSINGS!

My prayer is that the words I shared here from the ESV bible and my own experiences will be of assistance to some weary soul. I do not know all things biblical but am a willing student and I am willing to share life experiences honestly if it will help just one. God commands us to go out and share to word for his glory and I pray that the words of my mouth and the meditations of my heart are acceptable in his sight, oh Lord My strength and my redeemer.

God's Love and Blessings!

Angelia

Email: acvermen@yahoo.com

Websites:

http://angeliavernonmenchanserials.blogspot.com

http://acvermen.blogspot.com

WORDS FROM YOUR SISTER   Angelia Vernon Menchan

Notes and thoughts:

WORDS FROM YOUR SISTER   Angelia Vernon Menchan

Notes and Thoughts

WORDS FROM YOUR SISTER Angelia Vernon Menchan

Notesand
Thoughts_____
_____
_____
_____
_____
_____
_____
_____
_____
_____
_____

Notes and Thoughts:

WORDS FROM YOUR SISTER Angelia Vernon Menchan

WORDS FROM YOUR SISTER   Angelia Vernon Menchan

WORDS FROM YOUR SISTER   Angelia Vernon Menchan

Made in the USA
Charleston, SC
19 December 2014